PRACTICAL ABAP – DocB

A Practical Guide for Doc Builder

SELVA LAKSHMANAN

ISBN:0692446680
ISBN-13:9780692446683

Preface

This book is a practical ABAP guide focusing on document builder. The document builder is discussed more specific to SRM-PPS function. We believe that a practical ABAP guide that contains an explanation of related SAP configuration and business processes will be of great value to the developer.

From long experience in the SAP field, I am convinced that to be a highly sought after developer, you need a solid grounding of configuration concepts and technical elements that have a bearing on the ABAP objects you will be working on. The same applies to the functional consultant/configurator who should have at least a basic understanding of the various ABAP objects that influence a business process being designed.

The purpose of the book is to address the need for an integrated view of business process, configuration and ABAP code which will benefit both the configurator and the developer. The technical content of the book is intentionally kept at a beginner to intermediate level. This book is meant to be a guide for both the developer and functional analyst. This was not intended to be a step by step configuration manual or ABAP coding manual. Instead, it offers both a functional and technical perspective to the two groups that form the audience for this book. Depending on the context, we have explained underlying configuration, master data values or examples of business process throughout the book. Also, ABAP code samples have been given wherever appropriate.

We see that most organizations structure their SAP teams along these lines. It is quite likely that the ABAP developer will be exclusively attached to one of these teams or support all of these teams. The topics covered in this book will be very helpful to the ABAP developer by enhancing his knowledge of the business process.

Chapter 1, Overview explains the document builder features, process flow, DocB user and admin cockpit Web Dynpro. Chapter 2, Configuration explains Document builder configuration. Last chapter, Technical overview explains the details of the technical details, enhancements, Form integration, Application log, report and workflow.

This book is invaluable guid for ABAP developer and functional resource for document builder which integrates it with SRM-PPS module.

TABLE OF CONTENTS

1 Overview

The SAP Document Builder is a SAP generic tool to build and maintain the documents. SAP document builder is a content driven and cross-application solution powered by SAP NetWeaver 7.0 or higher.

Using Document Builder, You can generate simple to complex documents quickly and easily, using customer defined formats, templates, and clause content. It adds value to any business scenario that has a need to generate a complex document. The output format may be PDF, Microsoft World or XML. Latest version of the document builder is 3.0 and it supports web service and workflow enablement.

Document Builder is an optional component of SRM-PPS (Procurement for Public Sector). The latest version is Document Builder 3.0. You can generate complex documents for the Bid Invitation, Contract, Purchase Order, and Change Versions using the document builder. The main purpose of the book is that make you understand the basic functions of Document Builder and how it is integrated with SRM-PPS module.

SAP Document Builder integration is only provided by SRM-PPS for the contract, RFx, and purchase order business objects. If you want to integrate SAP Document Builder with other components, and if you want to support other business objects such as shopping carts, you must set up the integration yourself.

The chapter 2 covers the possible configuration and chapter 3 covers enhancements and Workflow for the document builder component.

1.1 Features

Document builder is one of business suite application and it has the following are basic functions:

- Customer-Configurable Document Structures (e.g., UCF), Layout, and Content (e.g., Clauses)

- Customer-Configurable Clause, Form, and Template Selection Logic
- Support for Full Text and In-By-Reference (IBR) Clauses
- Support for Clause Fill-ins by Government and Vendor Users
- Support for Standard Federal, Defense, Agency, and Custom Forms (i.e., SF, DD, OF, etc.)
- Automatic Import of Schedule (Section B), Line Items, and Key Data
- Ability to Update Clauses After a Change Version (i.e., Amendment or Modification)
- Ability to Retain Original Clauses or Update with Current Clauses (i.e., Clause History)
- Support for Clause Prescriptions, Agency Guidance, and Customer-Specific Local Guidance
- Support for Custom Clauses and Custom Text
- Integration with Adobe Document Server

1.2 Components

The document builder is based on Adobe server. The document builder requires the following components:

- SAP Document Builder is an add-on to SAP NetWeaver. You must have SAP NetWeaver 7.0 SP13 or higher, or SAP NetWeaver 7.1. SAP Document Builder requires the highest SAP NetWeaver support package.
- Adobe LiveCycle Designer ES - This component is optional. It is installed as an option in SAP GUI and is used to design Adobe PDF forms.
- Assembly server - This component is optional, as an assembly server is not required if you have opted for WordML or a simple XML output. An assembly server that generates a PDF file supports the XSL-FO transformation. For example, you may opt to use Adobe LiveCycle PDF Generator ES, Apache FOP, or another third party tool.
- SAP NetWeaver Application Server
- SAP NetWeaver Exchange Infrastructure - This component is not required if you have opted for a service-enabled environment

You can integrate Document Builder with other SAP and non-SAP applications. The basic document builder integration with SRM documents are Contract, RFx (Bid Invitation) and PO. You can integrate any other objects like Shopping Cart.

1.3 Process Flow

Document builder is a highly integrated component with SRM module. You can see the document builder link in the SRM document user interface. The link is available only for SRM-PPS component. You can access document builder UI to generate the document. In this section, you can see the process flow of the document builder integration.

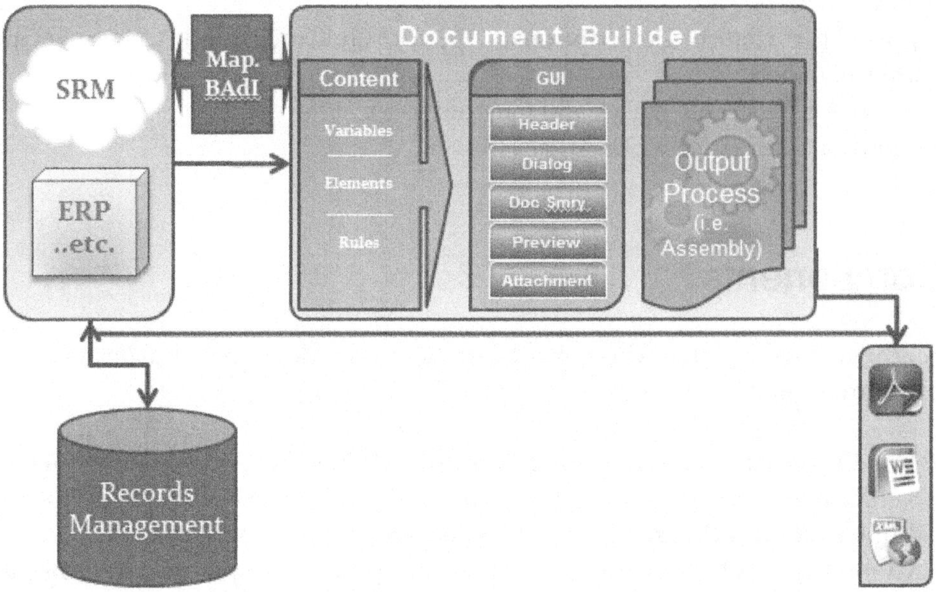

The process flow is defined as follows:

- SRM document PO, RFx or Contract is created in PPS functionality.
- A web service is used to call Document Builder.
- SRM data will be populated based on the configuration and enhancement to Document Builder.
- User can answer configured questions and verify and possible manipulation document summary data.
- Preview the document
- The element list can be either assembled in PDF or directly saved to WordML format.
- The final document is returned to the send application by means of Web services. You can also save the file to local PC/server or print or store it in records management.

SAP Document Builder is flexible and enables you to create documents in various formats. You can generate a PDF, an XML, a WordML, or a DOCX document. You can also generate combination of PDF and Microsoft Word documents, to meet your requirements. SAP Document Builder supports WordML and DOCX.

The following table lists the possible element and output formats and the required tools:

Element Format	**Output Format**	**Third-Party Tool**
Microsoft Word + Microsoft Word + Microsoft Word	Microsoft Word	Assembly: None required Editing: ActiveX Control for WordML only
Adobe Acrobat + Adobe Acrobat + Microsoft Word	Adobe Acrobat	Assembly: Adobe LiveCycle Editing: ActiveX Control for WordML only
HTML + HTML + Adobe Acrobat	Adobe Acrobat	Assembly: Adobe LiveCycle Editing: SAP BTF or third-party editor
HTML + HTML + HTML	Adobe Acrobat	Assembly: Apache FOP Editing: SAP BTF or third-party editor
XML + XML + XML	XML	Assembly: None required Editing: XML editor

1.4 User Interface

The document builder has a front UI cockpit to enter manual data entry and release the document to SRM document. The elements and clauses can be configured using the admin UI cockpit which is built by Web Dynpro Application /IPRO/WD_COCKPIT. The standard user document builder cockpit uses the Web Dynpro application /IPRO/WD_DOCB.

In SRM, Document Builder can be launched in three ways:

- Standalone – user directly executes the Document Builder Web Dynpro application.
- Externally to create a Document Builder session – for example, Document Builder is interfaced to SRM. SRM sends data to Document Builder to create/update a document, and opens a user session.
- Externally in the dark – Document Builder is the interface to an external system to create/update documents and return assembled documents with involving a user.

There are two parts to the end-user interface: the Document Builder UI (User Cockpit) and the Document Builder Cockpit (Admin Cockpit).

The user cockpit is used by the end-user and it is executed from related links in the SRM procurement UI screen. You can configure the standard elements and you need admin authorization to execute this transaction.

1.4.1 User Cockpit

The user cockpit is a Web Dynpro application and it is used to answer the configured questions and review and manipulate the document summary data. The user cockpit can be accessed from the Document builder link from SRM document screen. The user document builder cockpit has three main parts.

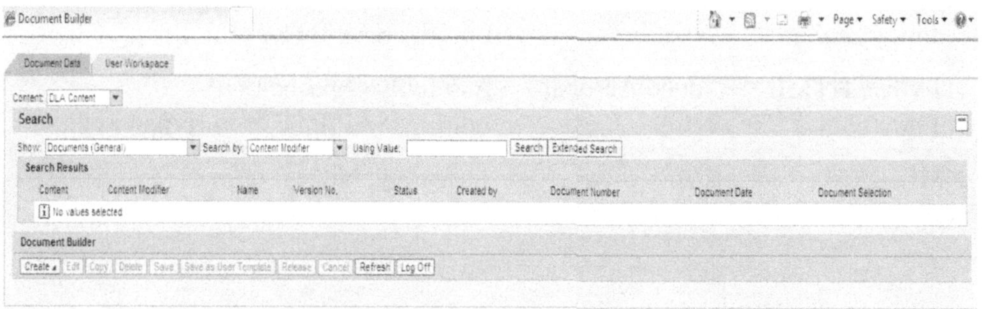

- **Search Area** - This area is applicable only when document builder is launched in stand-alone mode. You can do search on the documents. If the document builder is executed from the SRM screen then it will create or fetch the document directly and there is no other option to search or create the document.

- **Object Identification Area** (OIA). The OIA allows the user to search for and recall previously generated documents. The OIA area shows buttons like create, Save, Edit, Copy, Log Off, etc.

- **Action area** - This area is a collection of tab-strips including

- **Header area** – which allows the user to choose document version for previously created document, document selection and overlay for newly created documents. The header area has sections like General data, Regulation Sets, Document Versions and Administrative data.

- **Dialog area** – which allows the user to respond to Q&A questions. The dialog area process dynamically selects elements to be included in the document.

Questions based on the rules are displayed and subsequent questions are determined by previous answers. You can process the questions using Previous, Next, and, answer all questions with the default values from the selected template on Header data.

- **Element summary area** – represents an outline of the document by listing all elements to be included in the assembled document. Also, it allows you to manipulate the generated element list.

- **Preview area** – which allows the user to generate outputs, e.g. assemble the document, generate forms and reports, etc.

- **Attachment area** – which allows the user to attach external documents to the current Document Builder document

- **Workflow area** – which allows the user to route documents.

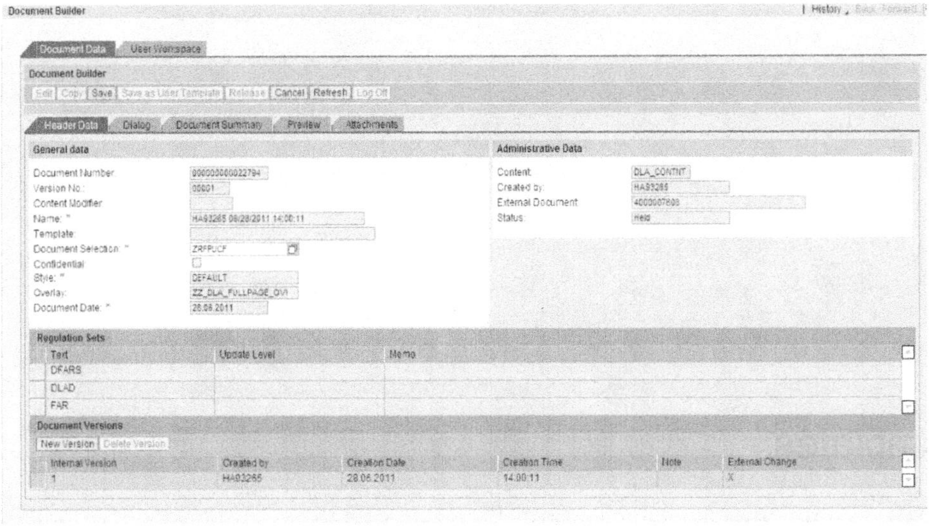

1.4.2 Admin Cockpit

Admin cockpit is a Web Dynpro application where you can create the standard elements. Note that you maintain the standard elements in IMG configuration. You can maintain elements in web interface rather than IMG. Also, you can edit text for the elements.

The following sample screenshots for the admin cockpit.

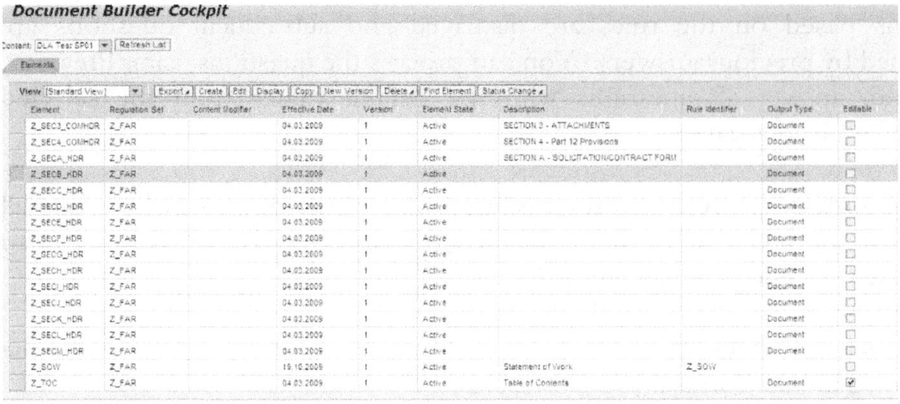

Editing clause.

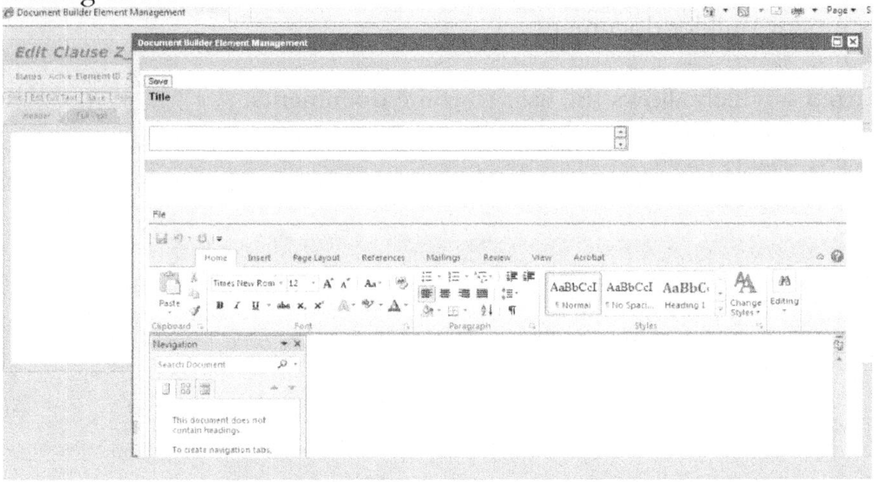

1.5 Templates

The template in Doc Builder is a reusable document that provides the structure and content to allow the user to avoid having to recreate the document every time. A template allows the ability to reuse a specified built list of dialog responses. When you open document builder to create a new terms and conditions document, you can pick the template from the header tab. The list of templates is listed in the template drop down.

All users will have access to set up and re-use templates. The templates will have their own naming convention. You can create templates in the stand alone document builder cockpit program. The template information is stored in the database table /IPRO/TTEMPL. The lock object for the template is /IPRO/E_TTEMPL.

1.6 Roles

The role is combination of more authorization objects with activities. You can assign a role to a user. Then the user will have all access defined in the role. You can assign multiple roles to a user. The role can assign to multiple users. You can create role using the transaction code PFCG.

You can create a composite role where you can assign one or more roles to a role. When you assign a composite role then all defined roles are assigned to the user. You cannot define any authorization object in the composite role. The role definition is part of SAP security team. SAP delivers a set of standard roles for the financial components level. You can define your own roles. Based on the user position, you can assign appropriate roles to the users.

The pre-defined roles for document builder are as follows:

- Content Manager (/IPRO/CONTENT_MANAGER)
- Professional Contract Author (/IPRO/PROF_CONTRACT_AUTHOR)
- Legal Contract Author (/IPRO/CONTRACT_AUTHOR)
- Contract Viewer (/IPRO/CONTRACT_VIEWER)
- Attribute Library Administrator (/IPRO/ATTR_LIBRARY_ADMIN)
- Clause Library Administrator (IPRO/CLAUSE_LIBRARY_ADMIN)
- Template Library Administrator (/IPRO/TMPL_LIBRARY_ADMIN)
- User / Author (/IPRO/AUTHOR)
- Group Manager (/IPRO/GROUP_MANAGER)
- Manager (/IPRO/ MANAGER)

2 Configuration

Document builder is a highly configurable module with wide range of configurable functions. You can implement document builder integration with minimal or no code using the DocB configuration. In this chapter, you will see that how to configure the basic document builder configuration. You can invoke the document builder configuration directly by the transaction /IPRO/DOCB_IMG.

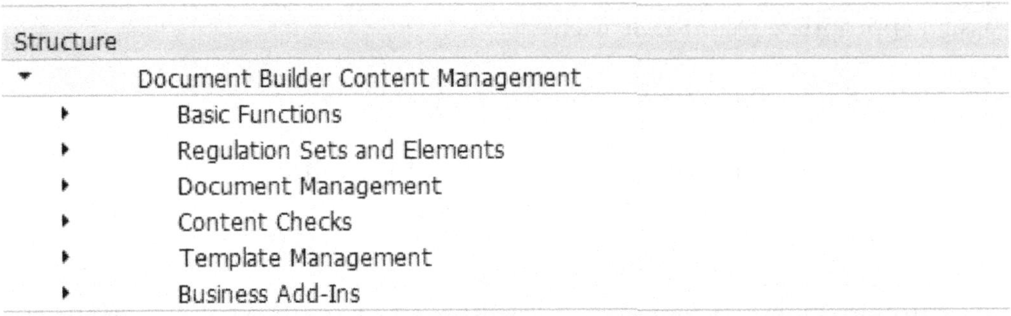

2.1.1 Activation

To use document builder, you must activate the document builder integration. You can activate the document builder at document types. You can access this IMG step by the IMG path SRM Server->Cross Industry Functions->Integration with SAP Document Builder->Activate Document Builder Integration.

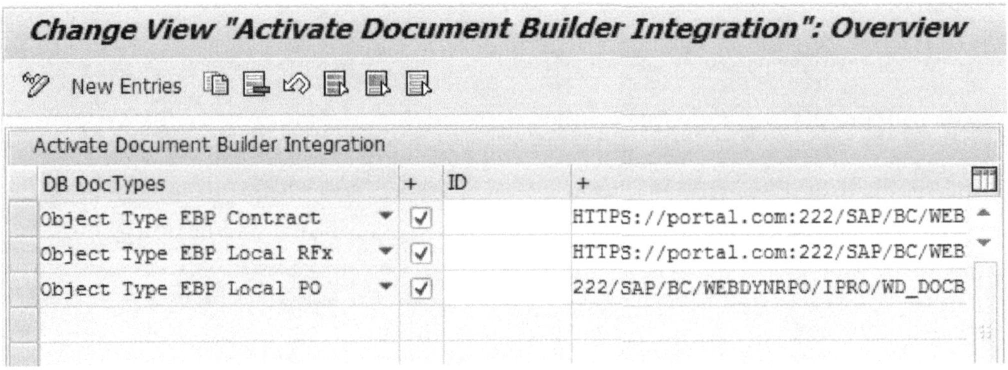

The allowed document types are Contract, Local PO and Local RFx. You must provide the User cockpit Web Dynpro URL Link. You can get URL link from Web Dynpro Application using SE80 or portal team.

2.2 Map Fields

Mapping fields integrates SRM data into SRM document builder. In the IMG configuration, you can map fields between SRM data variables into document builder variables. The configuration path is SRM Server->Cross Industry Functions->Integration with SAP Document Builder->Map fields.

Configured mapping fields will be stored in the transparent table /SAPPSSRM/DB_MAP. Note that the SRM variables can be selected for the different mapping types are part of the following structures:

Type	Description	Structure
01	Header	BBP_PDS_HEADER
02	Item	BBP_PDS_ITEM
03	Accounting	BBP_PDS_ACC
04	Organizational Unit	P1028 and P1000-STEXT
05	Purchasing Org.	P1028 and P1000-STEXT
06	Purchasing Group	P1028 and P1000-STEXT
10 - 27	Partner Data	BBP_PDS_PARTNER

To map SRM attributes to Document Builder simple variables, you need to specify the requested information viz., Object, Type, Attribute and DocB variable. Note that data is sent from SRM to Document Builder via an XML structure representative of the simple variables in Document Builder. This data can be accessed and modified during creation of the XML structure in SRM by activating enhancement spot /SAPPSSRM/DOCB_MAPPING. This enhancement spot is iteratively executed for each node and variable of XML structure. The DocB Mapping BADI is discussed in a later section.

2.3 Output Control

Output control is list of output control based on your business needs. You can access using IMG menu path SRM Server->Cross Industry Functions->Basic Functions->Output Control->Define Output Definition.

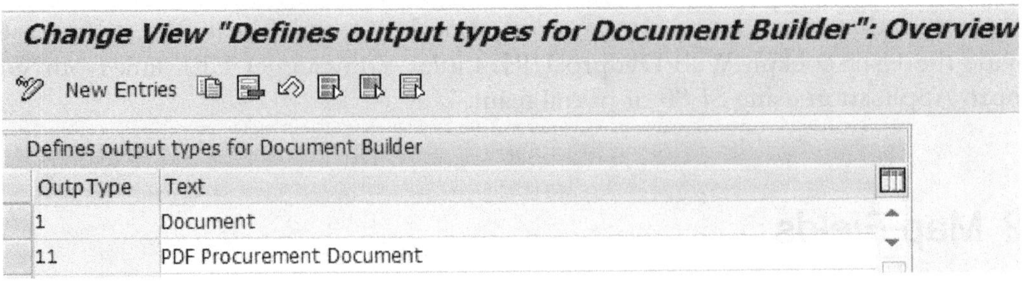

The BADI /IPRO/OUTPUT filters based on output control type. You can implement the BADI for each output type. The BADI will be discussed in the enhancement chapter.

2.4 Document Content

Document content establishment is the first step in configuring Document Builder. Document content is a container including Text for clauses, Evaluation rules for clauses, PDF forms and document styles. The document content is required for the subsequent configuration tasks. You can configure the contents using IMG path Basic function-> Define Contents.

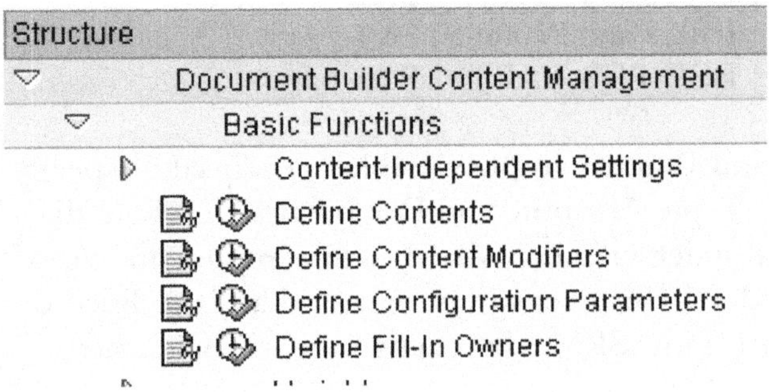

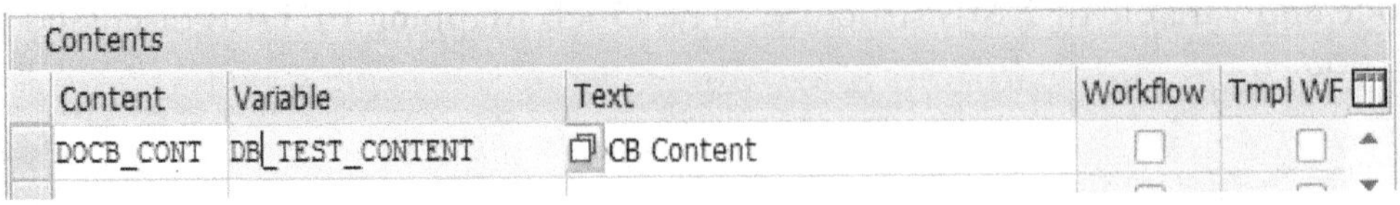

SAP supports more configurations on the document content.

2.4.1 Content Modifiers

You can define modifiers or variants to distinguish between contents. By implementing content modifiers, you can enable the system to support baseline content with an option to override defaults. That is, the system can contain base content shared by all in addition to features unique to each modifier. The modifier may have its own unique content to replace the base line. This applies to Elements, Guidance texts, Prescriptions for elements, variables, reference information for a variable and document selections. The content modifier is required configuration.

2.4.2 Configuration Parameters

You can configure the configuration parameters for document content. The configuration parameters include technical parameters and non-technical parameters used in the document assembly process. Due to the highly technical nature of the configuration parameters, it is strongly recommended that a System Administrator or qualified person perform this activity. The configuration path is Basic Functions->Define Configuration parameters.

Configuration Parameters

Configuration Parameter	Parameter Value
APPEND_NOTE	N
APP_LOG	X
CLS_TITLES_ON	Y
CLS_TITLE_LIST_LEVEL	1
CLS_TITLE_LIST_STYLE	SECTIONHEADERLIST
CLS_TITLE_NUMBERED	Y

The following are some pre-defined configuration parameters:

- ADS - Refers to the ADOBE Document Server, which is used for document assembly. The parameter value that gets entered is the LOGICAL DESTINATION. In this case the logical destination is SM59LC_ASSM2. Transaction SM59 (RFC Destinations (Display/Maintain)) is used to display and maintain the configuration of system RFC destinations.

- APP_LOG - Refers to the writing of error messages in the application log. Enter 'X' to write errors to the log. This is required in Notify Content Manager for Rules that cannot be Determined.

- CLS_TITLES_ON - Refers to an element title in a document. Enter 'Y' to display the title or 'N' to hide it.

- CLS_TITLE_LIST_LEVEL - Refers to the element title list level. This parameter works in conjunction with the SEC_TITLE_LIST_LEVEL parameter. Enter a numeric value, for example '1'.

- CLS_TITLE_LIST_STYLE - Refers to the element title list style. Enter a style name.
- CLS_TITLE_NUMBERED - Refers to the numbering of element titles. Enter 'Y' or 'N'.

- CLS_TITLE_TEXT_STYLE - Refers to a style for element title text style. Enter a style name.

- CM - Refers to the user name of the Content Manager. This setting enables you to send an e-mail to the CM inbox in the SAP Business Workplace (SBWP) when report Notify Content Manager for Rules that cannot be Determined is executed. The error reports may also be forwarded to a user's external e-mail address when the SBWP has been configured accordingly.

- FORMAT - Refers to the element format. This parameter and the associated value 'WORDML' are only required if you have opted for a solution based on Microsoft Word, that is, when you edit text in WordML. In addition to this parameter, the parameters listed below are required and must be defined as styles in an overlay document associated with content.

- LOG_SYS_SRM - Refers to the logical system where Document Builder is located and installed.

- LPCONFIG_LC_WORDML - This parameter is required if Adobe LiveCycle is used to assemble documents for contents that use WordML. The value is the logical port of the Document Builder LiveCycle client proxy for WordML assembly.

- SEC_TITLES_ON.- Refers to the section titles in a document. Enter 'Y' to display the titles or 'N' to hide them.

- SEC_TITLE_LIST_LEVEL - Refers to the section title list level. This parameter works in conjunction with the CLS_TITLE_LIST_LEVEL parameter. Enter a numeric value, for example '0'.

- SEC_TITLE_LIST_STYLE - Refers to the section title list style. Enter a style name.

- SEC_TITLE_NUMBERED - Refers to the numbering of sections. Enter 'Y' or 'N'.

- SEC_TITLE_TEXT_STYLE - Refers to the section title list style. Enter a style name.

- SYS_STYLES_OVERLAY - In Document Builder 3.0 SP02, the concept of the System Overlay was introduced to avoid issues with Document Builder editing the Microsoft Word 'NORMAL.DOT' file.

- TOC_SECTION - Refers to the section name in which you plan to have the element containing the table of contents (TOC) of the document. When the table of contents is generated in the assembled document, all sections having a document selection order number less than or equal to the order number of the section name entered in the TOC_SECTION parameter are ignored and excluded from the table of contents.

The configuration parameters are stored in the database table /IPRO/TCONFIG. You can read configuration parameter value from this table. You can define your own custom parameters in the configuration parameters and that can be used in your custom code.

2.4.3 Fill-in Owners

Fill-in owner is a variable attribute. The fill-in attribute is exclusively used for information purposes.

Owners

Fill-In Owner	Text
BOTH	Both (Government and Vendor)
GOVERNMENT	Government
VENDOR	Vendor

2.4.4 Variables

The variable is the lowest level item in document builder. A variable represents a dynamic piece of data that can be populated in a doc builder document (clause output or form), or can trigger logic within a rule. A variable can either pull data mapped from SRM or can be inputted from the end user in the fill-ins. You can enter fill-ins in dialog tree by selecting a node. Also, you can complete the Fill-ins values in the Document Summary tab of document builder. In summary tab, you can preview the responses from an end user and make updates or new entries. Only clauses that you have already been selected will populate its variables in the output document. If you are not selected a clause and, its variable is filled, the variables' content will not appear in the final output.

In SAP Document Builder, the following variable types are used:

- **Simple variables** - Simple variables are standalone variables. When a variable is used in the dialog process, each variable is actually a question that determines the contents of a document. Each variable can be linked to a reference help text, which is a part of a regulation set. Data can be mapped into a simple variable from an external source.

- **Structure variables** - Structure variables enable you to group variables according to functional similarity. Before defining variables, however, you must define a structure (or root variable) for the highest node in the Document Data Tree, which may contain dependent structures and simple variables. Once you have defined the root structure, you must perform the activity Define Contents and enter the newly defined root structure.

- **Table variables** - Table variables can be used for forms, reports and clause selection. Table variables are rendered in elements as tables, with each structure being a row. To create a table variable, you must create:
    - The simple variables it will contain
    - A structure
    - The table variable that specifies a name and key field for the table. You can insert the table variable into a standard element at a later stage.

The configuration of variables is a vital part of document builder. Identifying the variables is one of important document builder implementation. You can define the variables in IMG configuration. You can access this IMG activity using the path Basic Functions->Variables->Define Variables. You can create simple variables and structure the variables. Due to the high volume of variable entries, you are recommended that use naming conventions for variables. It helps you easier maintenance and retrieval of the variables.

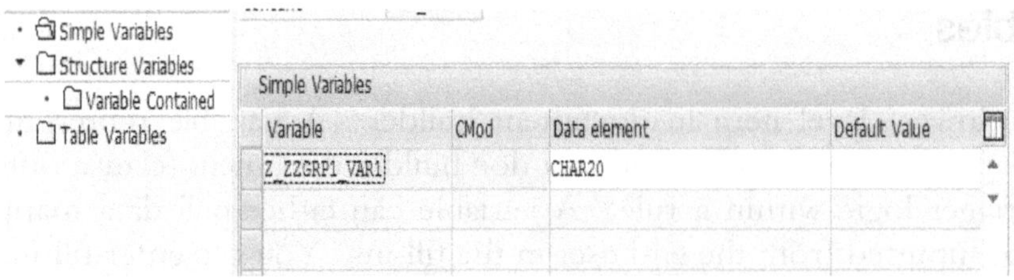

Note that you can create simple variables from SRM data. There is a standard SRM program /IPRO/READ_SRM_VARIABLES to create simple variables. You use the transaction /IPRO/READ_SRM_VAR to access this program. There is an IMG activity to execute this transaction. The program creates the variables for the attributes defined in the table /SAPPSSRM/DB_MAP.

You can link the variables with reference and regulation set. You can access this in IMG in the following path Basic Functions->Variables->Link References to Variables.

2.5 Regulation Set

The regulation set is a grouping of selected elements (including both clauses and forms). The regulation sets are listed on the header tab of the document after the template is selected and indicate the last updated date of any of the clauses within. You can configure the regulation sets and elements using the IMG menu path Cross-Application Components->Document Builder->Regulation Sets and Elements.->Define Regulation Sets. Instead of using standard SAP regulation sets, you can copy into new custom regulation sets for a cleaner configuration.

2.5.1 Elements

An element is the most basic level of content that is loaded in DocB. Typically, an element will represent a single clause, but it may also be a standard form. There are standard elements that were loaded from the SAP delivered FAR content. Elements refer to clauses, forms, reports and header/footer clauses. You can create the elements in HTML or in WordML. The IMG menu path is Cross-Application Components->Document Builder->Regulation Sets and Elements.->Define Regulation Sets->Standard Elements-> Define Elements.

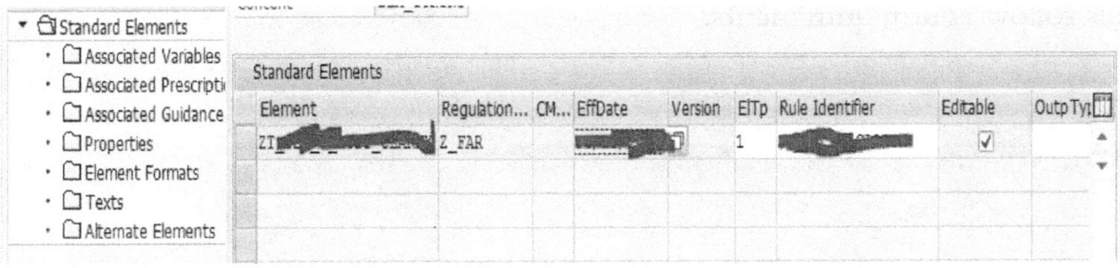

2.5.2 Rules

A rule is a Boolean logic statement that directs DocB to include a clause or exclude a clause. Rules are set up through the rule wizard in DocB. You can define rule to include a clause. You can named the rules typically same as (or close as) a clause. The rule will reference a variable or several variables to build the necessary logic. Rules can be previewed on the bottom of the Document Summary tab after highlighting the associated clause.

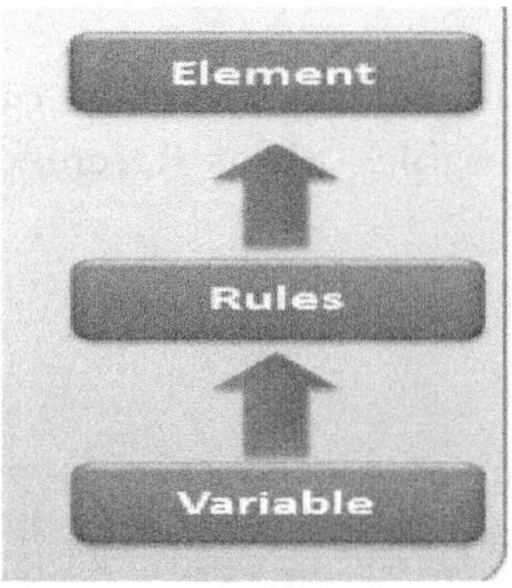

You can configure rules using the IMG path Document Builder->Regulation Sets and Elements->Rule Management->Define Rules.

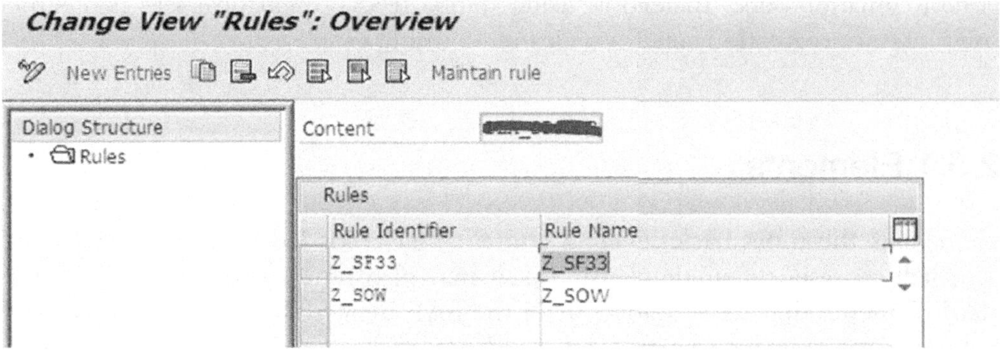

You can maintain rules' logic using the formula editor. The formula editor helps you to maintain rules with ease. You can use rules to include, exclude the element and you can set value for the element. You can define rule with any complexity. Make sure that rules follow your requirements.

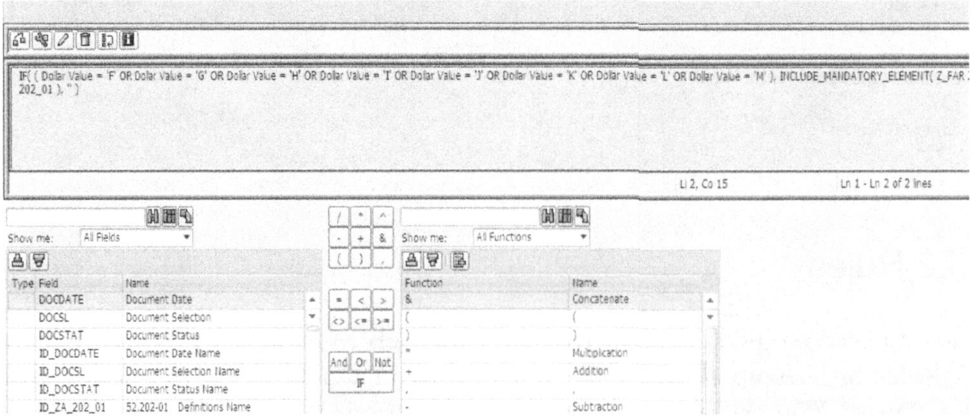

Rules can be nested and supports very complex logic. You can apply rules to any type of element, clause, form, report, etc. The rules are stored in the database table /IPRO/TRULES.

2.6 Document Structure

The Document Selection is the equivalent of Document Type in Doc Builder. The Doc Selection has the regulation sets mapped to it, and it also has the individual clauses mapped to it. The document selection is one of basic document builder configurations.

The following were pre-loaded from SAP and align with the FAR:

- CONCOM
- CONUCF
- MODUCF
- RFPCOM
- RPFUCF

A document consists of a collection of elements (or sections). For example, UCF documents have a structure different from construction documents. The solicitation UCF documents have a structure different from award UCF documents. The structure of document consists of the following configurable features:

- Document Type – You can define document types to distinguish documents in a particular area. For example, you can define document type for Bid Invitation, Contract and Information for Bid, etc. The configuration can be invoked in the path Document Management->Define Document Types. The information is stored in the table /IPRO/TDOCTYP.

Document Types

Doc Type	Text
Z_RFP	Request for Proposal
Z_RFQ	Request for Quote

- Document Format – You can define the document formats used by the client like Commercial or Uniform Contract Format. In the document format, you can define associated sections. You can structure the document format into sections. The configuration path is Document Management->Define Document Formats and Sections.

- Document Selection – In document selection, you can group document selections and to display only relevant information to Author. In the document grouping, you can combine document types and document formats uniquely to contain default properties such as style, overlay, sections and ordering. The document selection configuration is used for questions asked to author in UI cockpit. The document selection involves document group and document selection. The configuration path is Document Management->Document Group and Selection.

- Document Styles – You can define styles which include information about font, paragraph formatting, indent and other features. The configuration path is Content Independent Settings->Style Management->Define Styles.
- Document Overlay – You can define headers and footers for a doucment. The configuration path is Document Management->Define Overlay.

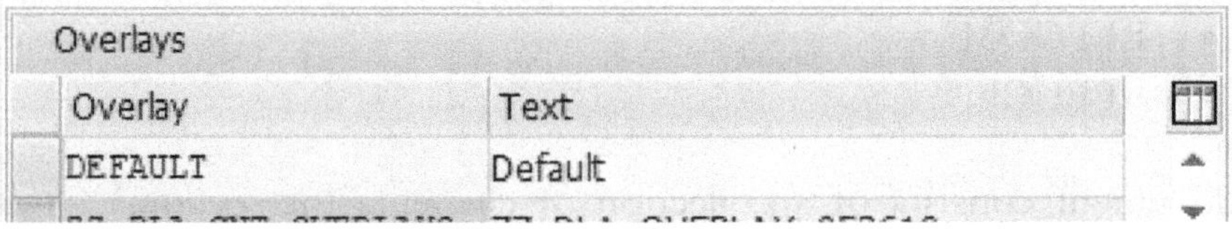

- Ordering – You can define ordering elements in overall or in a section. The configuration path is Document Management->Document Ordering->Define Ordering.

Note that document builder does not store the element content for any generated document. It simply stores the list of elements. The assembly process will generate the document using stored element list.

3 Technical Overview

Document builder provides a set of technical objects for the document builder technical framework. This section explains the document content, document, versions, document data and document actions with some sample code. The technical overview also includes authorization object and Workflow information

Document builder is a highly configurable component. Some of complex customer requirements cannot be covered in basic configuration. SAP document builder provides a number of enhancement (BADIs) to enhance document builder technical solution. In this chapter, we are discussing the ABAP objects and possible enhancements and explained with technical challenges and solutions.

3.1 Web Services

Document uses web services to read the variables value. The web service proxy is purely based on the variables definition. The web service uses the WSDL which is generated based on the variables definition. So, you need to modify the web service proxy when there is any change in the variables definition. You may need to change variables and sometime it is an on-going activity. For example, you need to delete variables (no other changes) then SAP recommends that do not delete any unwanted variables. Instead of deleting, you can set the variable(s) in inactive status to negate the need to re-generate Proxy WSDL. You can create/maintain the client proxy using the transaction se80.

3.2 Base Objects

Document builder supports a number of ABAP objects and function modules. In this section, you are going through the technical details for base document builder objects. SAP delivers a number of ABAP class objects for the document builder. The object name starts with '/IPRO/CL_'. All the table names start with /IPRO/T_ and view name starts /IPRO/V_.

The following are list of few important document builder tables.

Table Name	Description
/IPRO/TDOCMNT	Document builder documents
/IPRO/TDOCSL	Document selection
/IPRO/TCONTENT	Content types
/IPRO/TDOCST	Document status
/IPRO/TCONFIG	Document Builder Configuration Parameters
/IPRO/TDOCEXPIRE	Document Expiration Thresholds
/IPRO/TDOCDATA	XML Document Data
/IPRO/TDOCTYP	Contains data for document type
/IPRO/TELMNT	Element table
/IPRO/TNOTE	DocB Element Note Table
/IPRO/TACTION	Authorization Actions
/IPRO/TATTACH	Document Builder Attachments
/IPRO/TDOCUSR	Users that can access the document
/IPRO/TELM_VAR	Association between elements and variables -- fill-in vars
/IPRO/TOUTDEF	Defines output types for Document Builder
/IPRO/TOUTPUT	Further defines output in Document Builder
/IPRO/TOVERLY	Table for ADS overlays of document headers and footers
/IPRO/TRGSET	Regulation Set table
/IPRO/TRULES	Element Rules Description
/IPRO/TTMPLDATA	Table for storing template data in XML format

3.2.1 DocB Document

The DocB document is a single document record. The document is uniquely referred by GUID. The class interface /IPRO/IF_DOCUMENT is used for DocB document. There is a factory class /IPRO/IF_DOCB_FACTOR available to handle the DocB document. You can access the DocB document content using this factory. The following section explains technical details of DocB document.

The document header information is stored in the database table /IPRO/TDOCMNT. The SRM document object ID is stored in the column ext_doc_id. The table has a unique GUID (DOCMNT) and document number is stored in the column docmnt_id which can be used to retrieve the document. The following is sample code to access the DocB document.

```
DATA:
  lo_docb_factory TYPE REF TO /ipro/if_docb_factory,
  lo_document     TYPE REF TO /ipro/if_document.
.......
  READ TABLE lt_contents INTO lo_content INDEX 1.
```

```
IF lo_content IS BOUND.
 lo_docb_factory = lo_content->get_docb_factory( ).
 lo_document ?= lo_docb_factory->open(
            piv_docmnt = iv_docmnt).
ENDIF.
```

The interface class /IPRO/IF_DOCB_ATTRIBUTE is used to manage DOCB document attributes. The document attributes have a number of methods like add, remove, & lookup the node, get parent and child nodes and get & set the value. The following sample code to get all simple variables from the document data and how to set the variable.

```
DATA: lo_document_data    TYPE REF TO /ipro/if_docb_attribute,
  lt_simple_vars       TYPE /ipro/tt_attributes,
  lo_versions         TYPE REF TO /ipro/if_docb_attribute,
  lo_simple_var       TYPE REF TO /ipro/if_docb_attribute.
TRY.
  lo_versions = eo_document->/ipro/if_versions~get_versions( ).
*    io_document->/ipro/if_action~switch_mode( 'U' ).
  lo_document_data = io_document->get_document_data( ).
  lt_simple_vars = lo_document_data->get_children( iv_leaves_only = 'X'
                                        iv_deep        = 'X' ).
 CATCH /ipro/cx_attribute_paramerr
       /ipro/cx_action_noauth INTO lo_exception.
ENDTRY.
LOOP AT lt_simple_vars INTO lo_simple_var.
  lv_simple_var_name = lo_simple_var->get_name( ).
  CASE lv_simple_var_name.
    WHEN 'ZVAR_NAME1'.
     lo_simple_var->set( lv_var_name ).
  ENDCASE.
ENDLOOP.
```

Document builder supports version management. You can have multiple versions for a DocB document. From technical perspective, the DocB document version has a separate interface class /IPRO/IF_VERSIONS and it is interfaced in the interface class /IPRO/IF_DDOCUMENT. You can create, remove, set and get current version and activate the version as a new active version.

Document header is also one of the document attributes and it can be assigned to /IPRO/DOCB_ATTRIBUTE. The document header can be retrieved by GET_DOCUMENT_DATA method.

In SRM PPS, the document builder document id is stored in the PS_DOCB_ID of the header structure. If the document builder is integrated with a SRM object type then you can see the associated document builder document in the field PS_DOCB_ID.

The lock object for the DocB document is /IPRO/E_TDOCMNT. The following code is to lock a DocB document.

```
CALL FUNCTION 'ENQUEUE_/IPRO/E_TDOCMNT'
EXPORTING
mode_/ipro/tdocmnt       = 'E'
mode_/ipro/tdocdata      = 'E'
mandt                   = sy-mandt
docmnt                  = lv_docmnt_guid
*  X_DOCMNT                 = ' '
*  _SCOPE                  = '2'
*  _WAIT                  = ' '
*  _COLLECT                 = ' '
EXCEPTIONS
foreign_lock             = 1
system_failure           = 2
OTHERS                   = 3  .
```

3.2.2 Document Content

The document content is stored in the table /IPRO/TCONTENT. You can access the document contents using FM /IPRO/CONTENT_FACTORY. If the content name is not specified then the function picks all the contents defined in the configuration. The function module implements the class interface /IPRO/IF_CONTENT. You can view the interface implementation code in the function group. Note that the implementation is in local class. The methods like GET_USER_ELEMENTS, GET_USER_TEMPLATES, GET_CONFIGS, etc. are implemented.

```
DATA:
 lv_content     TYPE string,
 lt_contents    TYPE /ipro/tt_contents.

    CALL FUNCTION '/IPRO/CONTENT_FACTORY'
     EXPORTING
      piv_name     = lv_content
     IMPORTING
      pet_contents = lt_contents.
```

You can access the content object from DocB object.

```
lo_content = lo_docb->get_content( ).
```

3.2.3 Element

The document element is referred by the interface /IPRO/IF_DOCB_ELEMENT. The document section is referred by the interface /IPRO/IF_DOCB_SECTION. The lock object for the Eleement is /IPRO/E_TELMNT. The following sample code shows you how to handle elements and sections.

```
DATA: lo_elm_list     TYPE REF TO /ipro/if_docb_attribute,
       lo_elements     TYPE REF TO /ipro/if_docb_element,
      lo_elm_section  TYPE REF TO /ipro/if_docb_section,
      lt_elms         TYPE /ipro/tt_attributes,
lo_elm_list = Lo_document->get_element_list( ).
lt_elms = lo_elm_list->get_children( iv_deep = 'X' ).
LOOP AT lt_elms INTO lo_elm_list.
  TRY.
   lo_elm_section ?= lo_elm_list.
  CATCH cx_dynamic_check.  " There are no sections, only elements
   IF ( lo_elm_section IS NOT INITIAL ).
     FREE lo_elm_section.
   ENDIF.
  ENDTRY.
ENDLOOP.
```

3.2.4 Document Action

Action is an activity that you can perform on the document builder document. The activity is one of document object attribute and it is referred by the interface class /IPRO/IF_ACTION. The following methods are available.

Method	Description
PROCESS	Process DocB business Logic
POST	Post an active document
HOLD	Hold the document
IS_ACTION_ALLOWED	Determine a certain action is allowed.
COMPLETE	Release a document
RELEASE	Release a document
CREATE_VERSION	Create a new version

The following is sample code that force to release DocB document.

```
* Get DOCb document
 TRY.
   lo_content = io_document->get_content( ).
   io_document->/ipro/if_action~finish_with_defaults( ).
   io_document->/ipro/if_action~process( ).
```

```
      io_document->/ipro/if_action~post( ).
      lo_content->commit( ).
    CATCH /ipro/cx_action_illegal
        /ipro/cx_action_foreign_lock
        /ipro/cx_action_status
        /ipro/cx_action_noauth
        /ipro/cx_attribute_illegal
        /ipro/cx_attribute_type INTO lo_exception.
      ev_ret          = gc_error_post_form.
      ev_error_string = lo_exception->if_message~get_text( ).
      CONCATENATE 'Error' ev_error_string
       INTO ev_error_string RESPECTING BLANKS SEPARATED BY space.
  ENDTRY.
```

The following is the sample code to generate PDF file from the document builder.

```
TRY.
  lt_output_types = io_docb->/ipro/if_output~get_output_types( ).
  lv_output_type = '11'.
  io_docb->/ipro/if_output~enable( piv_type = lv_output_type ).
  ls_output = io_docb->/ipro/if_output~generate(
              piv_type = lv_output_type ).
  lv_pdf_xstring = ls_output-data.
    CATCH cx_root INTO lo_root.
      WRITE:/ 'Error generating the document'.
ENDTRY.
  CALL FUNCTION 'SCMS_XSTRING_TO_BINARY'
    EXPORTING
      buffer    = lv_pdf_xstring
    TABLES
      binary_tab = lt_data.
* Use GUI_DOWNLOAD FM to download the lt_data into PDF or binary file
```

3.2.5 Function Modules

There are number of function modules associated with DocB. The few of useful function modules are listed below.

Function Module	Comments
/IPRO/VIEW_PDF	Viewing PDF content
/IPRO/VIEW_MIME	Viewing MIME content
/IPRO/EDIT_HTML	Launch BTF editor to view/edit HTML
/IPRO/SAVE_DOCUMENT	Save the document

/IPRO/CHECKIN_DOCUMENT	Check in the document
/IPRO/DOCUMENT_SEARCH	Search string in the document and returns the list of matched documents
/IPRO/LOCK_DOCUMENT	Lock the DocB Document
/IPRO/UNLOCK_DOCUMENT	Unlock the DocB Document
/IPRO/WFL_START	Start the workflow
/IPRO/CALL_DOCB_SYNCHRONOUS	RFC wrapper to call DocB
/IPRO/CLASSIF_GENERATE	Generate characteristics and classes
/IPRO/CHECKIN_DOCUMENT	Check in Document
/IPRO/CHECKOUT_DOCUMENT	Check out Document
/IPRO/DOCUMENT_SEND	Send Document to XI via Proxy
/IPRO/DOCUMENT_SERVICES	Document Services
/IPRO/APPLOG_CONTROL	App log control

3.3 Enhancement

Business Add-In (BADI) is an enhancement technique based on ABAP objects. BADI is an anticipated point of extension or well-defined interface in the source code to do enhancements. There are two types of BADI supported by SAP viz., classic and kernel-based BADIs. Kernel BADIs are highly integrated directly in ABAP runtime environment. Kernel BADIs are highly flexible and faster than classic BADI. The navigation screens are different between classic and kernel BADIs. You can list the BADIs using the transaction code SE94. Note that Document BADIs are prefixed with /IPRO or /SAPPSSRM.

SRM has two components BADI Definition and BADI Implementation. SAP provides the definition and you can implement the code for standard SAP BADI. You can define your own custom BADI also. You can access BADI definition using the transaction code SE18 and implementation using the transaction code SE19.

The important attributes of BADIs are multiple-use and BADI filter. The BADI filter is implementation will be executed based on the filter value at runtime environment. So, you can implement a separate implementation for each filter value combination. You can implement more than one implementation when the BADI has set to multi-use flag. When you do multiple implementations, make sure that each implement is not dependent on each other. The sequence of implementation is based on compilation. So, there is possible that you can have different sequence of implementations between development and Test or Product landscapes.

3.3.1 Activation BADI

You can activate the document builder integration using the IMG configuration. SRM provides a BADI where you can deactivate the document builder integration. The following technical challenge provides implementation of the dynamic activation of document builder integration.

Technical Challenge: The document builder is activated using the IMG configuration. For instance, the customer requirement is to turn off the document builder integration for the particular document types of PO. Also, the automatic PO sourcing requires no document builder. The PO will be created and ordered when PR is transferred from ECC back-end system.

Solution: Note that this solution is only applicable when document builder integration is activated in the system. When SRM data is passed to document builder, it always validates when integration is activated and there is a BADI /SAPPSSRM/DOCB_BADI to overwrite the document builder integration. To build the solution, you need to implement this BADI. The BADI has interface with Document object type and PD header detail. The changing parameter CV_DB_ACTIVE determines whether it is active or inactive.

Name: /SAPPSSRM/DOCB_BADI	Multiple Use: No	Filter: No
Description: Deactivates document builder integration.		

Method: SET_DOCB_INACTIVE
Description: Deactivate the Document Builder Integration.
Parameters:

Name	Type	Data Type	Description
IV_OBJECT_TYPE	Import	/SAPPSSRM/_OBJECT_TYPE	Object Type
IS_HEADER	Import	BBP_PDS_HEADER	Header
IV_CALLER	Import	CHAR10	String
CV_DB_ACTIVE	Change	SEU_BOOL	Active Flag

```
if iv_object_type = 'BUS2201'.
  call function 'SYSTEM_CALLBACK'
    EXPORTING
      max_level  = 100
    IMPORTING
      et_callstack = lt_callback.
  READ TABLE lt_callback TRANSPORTING NO FIELDS
   WITH KEY eventname = 'BBP_BS_SC_TRANSFER_SOURCING'.
   IF sys-subrc EQ 0.
        ev_db_inactive = 'X'.
   ENDIF.
endif.
if is_header-process_type = 'ZPRC'.
        ev_db_inactive = 'X'.
```

```
endif.
```

Note that SYSTEM_CALLBACK will return the ABAP stack. The event BBP_BS_SC_TRANFER_SOURCING is in the ABAP stack when the BADI is triggered from transfer program.

3.3.2 Mapping BADI

The Mapping between SRM data and variables can be configured in IMG. The BADI /SAPPSSRM/DOCB_MAPPING provides the option to override the variables for the assembled document builder. The BADI is executed on each variable setup. The BADI interface option to change XML node. You can change the variable value by setting value at Node. You can update any child node under the node.

Name: /SAPPSSRM/DOCB_MAPPING		Multiple Use: Yes	Filter: No
Description: Mapping for Synchronous Document Builder Integration.			
Method: CHANGE_MAPPING Description: Change Mapping. Parameters:			
Name	Type	Data Type	Description
IV_GUID	Import	GUID	GUID
IV_OBJECT_TYPE	Import	CHAR10	Object Type
IV_MODE	Import	CHAR1	Mode
IV_SAVE	Import	XFLAG	Save Flag
CO_NODE	Change	IF_IXML_NODE	XML Node
lv_var_name = co_node->get_name( ). TRANSLATE lv_var_name TO UPPER CASE. *Based on the variable, you can set your value lv_subrc = co_node->set_value(lv_new_value).			

Note that you can use get_next of co_node will give next available child node. You can do all changes at root level itself.

3.3.3 Output BADI

The BADI /IPRO/OUTPUT is executed whenever the document is assembled. The output generation is possible when DocB release or preview the document. You can implement the configured output types. You can change the data or mime type of the returning parameter PRS_OUTPUT. You can get all base information from PIR_DOCUMENT. The implementation is discussed in the Adobe form integration section.

3.3.4 Element Definition BADI

The BADI /IPRO/ELMNT_DEF is used to define what application to view or edit different type of clauses. SAP provides default implementation to use Business Text Framework (BTF) to edit the clauses in HTM or HTML clauses. The default form edit is SFP. The implementation is /IPRO/ELMNT_IMP.

```
method /IPRO/IF_EX_ELMNT_DEF~FORM_EDITOR.
  SET PARAMETER ID 'FPWBFORM' FIELD cv_form.
  CALL TRANSACTION 'SFP'.
  GET PARAMETER ID 'FPWBFORM' FIELD cv_form.
endmethod.
```

```
method /IPRO/IF_EX_ELMNT_DEF~LAUNCH_EDITOR.

  DATA: flag TYPE boolean,
      l_newtext TYPE xstring, action TYPE c.
  CLEAR ev_changed.
  CASE iv_format.
   WHEN 'HTML' OR 'HTM'.
    CALL FUNCTION '/IPRO/EDIT_HTML'
     EXPORTING
      iv_source   = iv_fulltext
      iv_mode     = iv_mode
      iv_title    = iv_title
     IMPORTING
      ev_text     = ev_string
      ev_cancel   = flag
     CHANGING
      cv_encoding = cv_encoding.
    IF flag = '' AND iv_mode = 'E'.
     ev_changed = 'X'.
    ENDIF.
   WHEN OTHERS.
    DATA: ls_txtfmt  TYPE /ipro/ttxtfmt,
        lv_type    TYPE string,
        lv_subtype TYPE string.
* Check for a supported format.
    SELECT SINGLE * FROM /ipro/ttxtfmt
     INTO ls_txtfmt
     WHERE txtfmt EQ iv_format.
    IF sy-subrc EQ 0.
     SPLIT ls_txtfmt-content_type AT '/' INTO lv_type lv_subtype.
* let user choose the action first
     IF iv_mode = 'E'.
      CALL FUNCTION '/IPRO/ELMNT_PRE_EDIT'
       IMPORTING
```

```
          ev_text   = l_newtext
          ev_action = action.
        CHECK action = 'O'.
        IF l_newtext IS INITIAL.
         l_newtext = iv_fulltext.
         ev_changed = ''.
        ELSE.
         ev_changed = 'X'.
         ev_string = l_newtext.
        ENDIF.
      ELSE.
       l_newtext = iv_fulltext.
       ev_changed = ''.
      ENDIF.
      CALL FUNCTION '/IPRO/VIEW_MIME'
       EXPORTING
        iv_title   = iv_title
        iv_content = l_newtext
        iv_type = lv_type
        iv_subtype = lv_subtype.
    ELSE.
      RAISE EXCEPTION TYPE /ipro/cx_invalid_format.
    ENDIF.
  ENDCASE.
endmethod.
```

3.3.5 Client Proxy BADI

The BADI /IPRO/CALL_SYNC_PROXY handles external sync proxies for DocB token handling. The BADI is triggered while commit the DocB changes. The implementation /IPRO/SRM_SYNC_INTEGRATION is delivered as part of SRM-PPS. SRM-PPS delivers proxy class /IPRO/CO_PSSRM_WS_DOCUMENT_TOK. The function module /SAPPSSRM/GET_TOKEN_FOR_DOCB handle the same. Also, the class /IPRO/CO_PSSRM_DOCB_ATTACH supports send attachment to the corresponding document.

Technical Challenge: SRM-PPS provides option to attach the file into the related procurement document. The requirement is that attachment file should be <object_type>_<object_id>_<object variable>.pdf. The object variable should be picked the value from variable Z_<object_type>_FORMNAME.

Solution: You need to implement the BADI /IPRO/CALL_SYNC_PROXY. Since, SRM-PPS already implemented an implementation. You need to deactivate the existing one and create new implementation. Copy the code of the method TOKEN and SEND_ATTACHMENTS. In the SEND_ATTACHMENTS method, you need to modify the file name attribute of the attachment.

<table>
<tr><td colspan="2">Name: /IPRO/CALL_SYNC_PROXY</td><td colspan="2">Multiple Use: No</td><td>Filter: No</td></tr>
<tr><td colspan="5">Description: /IPRO/CALL_SYNC_PROXY</td></tr>
<tr><td colspan="5">Method: TOKEN
Description: Token Handling
Parameters:</td></tr>
<tr><td>Name</td><td>Type</td><td>Data Type</td><td colspan="2">Description</td></tr>
<tr><td>PIV_PROXY_NAME</td><td>Import</td><td>SRT_LP_PROXY CLASS</td><td colspan="2">Proxy class of Logical port</td></tr>
<tr><td>PIV_LOGICAL_PORT</td><td>Import</td><td>SRT_LP_NAME</td><td colspan="2">Logical port</td></tr>
<tr><td>PIV_DOCUMENT</td><td>Import</td><td>GUID</td><td colspan="2">DocB Guid</td></tr>
<tr><td>PIV_CONTENT</td><td>Import</td><td>/IPRO/CONTENT</td><td colspan="2">Content</td></tr>
<tr><td>PIV_EXT_DOCID</td><td>Import</td><td>CHAR10</td><td colspan="2">Externeral document no</td></tr>
<tr><td>PIV_EXT_OBJID</td><td>Import</td><td>CHAR10</td><td colspan="2">External object type</td></tr>
<tr><td>PEV_TOKEN</td><td>Export</td><td>XFELD</td><td colspan="2">Flag</td></tr>
<tr><td colspan="5">*Copy same code of SRM-PPS implementation</td></tr>
<tr><td colspan="5">Method: SEND_ATTACHMENTS
Description: Send attachment to external system
Parameters:</td></tr>
<tr><td>Name</td><td>Type</td><td>Data Type</td><td colspan="2">Description</td></tr>
<tr><td>PIV_DOCUMENT</td><td>Import</td><td>GUID</td><td colspan="2">DocB Guid</td></tr>
<tr><td>PIV_CONTENT</td><td>Import</td><td>/IPRO/CONTENT</td><td colspan="2">Content</td></tr>
<tr><td>PIV_PROXY_NAME</td><td>Import</td><td>SRT_LP_PROXY CLASS</td><td colspan="2">Proxy class of Logical port</td></tr>
<tr><td>PIO_DOCUMENT</td><td>Import</td><td>/IPRO/IF_DOCUM ENT</td><td colspan="2">DocB interface</td></tr>
<tr><td>PEV_MESSAGE</td><td>Export</td><td>BAPIRET2</td><td colspan="2">Return parameter</td></tr>
<tr><td colspan="5">*Copy SRM-PPS code
* Make changes at LOOP AT lt_output_type before APPEND ls_srm_att to lt_srm_att
* Get object type and object id
  po_docb_document->get_document_header_fields(
      IMPORTING prs_doc_detail = lv_pr_doc).
  lv_object_id = lv_pr_doc-ext_doc_id.
  lv_object_type = lv_pr_doc-ext_object_id.
* Get form variable
 concatenate lv_object_type ‘FORM_NAME’ INTO lv_var_name
   separated by ‘_’.
 lo_doc_var = po_docb_document->get_document_data( ).
 lo_var = lo_doc_var->lookup(iv_name = lv_var_name).
 lo_var->get(importing e_data = lv_frm_name).
 concatenate lv_object_type ‘_’ lv_object_id ‘_’ lv_frm_name ‘.pdf’
    INTO ls_srm_att-filename.
append ls_srm_att into lt_srm_att.</td></tr>
</table>

You can use SEND_ATTACHMENTS to check any additional validations and raise the error message in the return parameter PEV_MESSAGE. You can implement if the variable Z_<object_type>_FORMNAME is not defined then you can raise the error message.

When you deactivate this BADI, the rendered document will not be sent to the SRM procurement document.

3.3.6 Other BADIs

- /IPRO/ORDER_DEF – You can use this BADI to determine whether a clause precede another clause ordering. SAP delivers default implementation /IPRO/ORDER_IMP to preceding logic.
- /IPRO/TEXT_SRCH_DEF – The BADI enables you to determine the methods that search substrings inside full text. SAP provides default implementation /IPRO/TEXT_SRCH_IMPL.
- /IPRO/ASSEMBLY_DEF – You can use this BADI to generate a document, form or schedule.
- /IPRO/RGSET_DEF - Determines a different collection of regulation sets used for creating Document Builder documents.
- /IPRO/GROUP_MANAGER - Enhances the Group Manager authorizations. This BADI will add extra authority check only. You cannot override the authorization failure.
- /IPRO/RULES - Enhances the Formula Builder used for defining rules.
- /IPRO/NAME_VALIDATOR - Determines how an element or a variable name is validated.
- /IPRO/LABEL_CHANGE - Changes the labels and tooltips of the buttons, tab-strips, and element status in SAP Document Builder.
- /IPRO/FILTER_GUID - Determines which guidance text(s) should be displayed on the SAP Document Builder user interface for an element depending on content or content modifier values.
- /IPRO/DETERMINE_BR- Builds the by-reference text for an element from the full-text of the element.

- /IPRO/INSERT_ELM - Determines whether or not an element should be inserted into a document.

- /IPRO/RUN_RULE - Determines whether a rule linked to an element should run depending on the element's inclusion status.

- /IPRO/ACTIONS – You can use this BADI to implement additional functions such as saving documents in SAP Records Management. The BADI is called via the user interface. The BADI implementation is based on filter value on content type (values are based on configuration) and object type (D – document, T – template, etc). The BADI has the following methods and all methods the /IRPO/IF_DOCUMENT interface is passed as import parameter. You can access the document information and do the subsequent functions.

    - HOLD – Hold document
    - POST – Post document
    - RELEASE – Release document
    - DELETE – Delete document
    - CREATE – Create document
    - REJECT – Reject document

- /IPRO/FM_ACTIONS – This BADI enables you to implement additional functions for the DocB actions via Web Service or RFC. It supports the following methods.

    - RELEASE – Release document
    - SAVE – Save document
    - CHECKIN – Check in document
    - CHECKOUT – Check out document
    - DELETE – Delete document
    - SERVICES – Document services

- /IPRO/ELEMENT_ACTION – You can use this BADI to enhance the action for elements. The BADI supports the 'Hold' action for document builder element. The BADI is called when the elements are saved or released.

- /IPRO/COLLABORATION – This BADI is called in the function module /IPRO/GET_COLLABORATION_DATA. SAP delivers the standard implementation /IPRO/COLLAORATION.

- /IPRO/EDITOR – The BADI allows you to replace the BTF editor (default editor in Document Builder) with another one. SAP delivers the standard implementation /IPRO/EDITOR. This is single use BADI.

- /IPRO/MATERIAL – You can use this BADI to distinguish major changes from minor changes in a released document. The minor change does not require any workflow approval. SAP delivers the standard implementation /IPRO/MATERIAL_IMP.

- /IPRO/NUMGEN – This BADI allows you to insert custom data into a document builder description header field.

- /IPRO/UI_CHANGES_WFL – This BADI allows you to change workflow screens like hide or display buttons. The BADI has the following methods and method returns the parameter RV_IS_VISIBLE. If the parameter is set then it displays the button.

    - SET_APPR_REPLACE_BUTTON – Set approver replace button
    - SET_REV_REPLACE_BUTTON – Set reviewer replace button
    - SET_REV_DELETE_BUTTON – Set reviewer delete button

- /IPRO/EXTERNAL_DATA – You can use this BADI to retrieve data from external systems such as SAP SRM or SAP CRM. SAP delivers the standard implementation /IPRO/EXTERNAL_DATA_IMP.

3.4 Form Integration

Forms and Reports are an integral part of document content and can be inserted into complex contract documents. As you know forms are elements and can be configured in the IMG configuration. SF26 Award data, SF30 Amendment and modification forms are good examples. To implement these forms, you must design the forms either in Smart Form or Adobe Forms. The Adobe form can be designed using the transaction SFP. Adobe form is an interactive form and it allows user to enter the data on the form whereas Smart Form is a static form. The step-by-step instructions are defined for integrating a new Adobe form with document builder.

- Generate WSDL file using the IMG activity Basic Functions->Variables->Information Systems-> Display output as WSDL or transaction /IPRO/OUTPUT_WSDL.

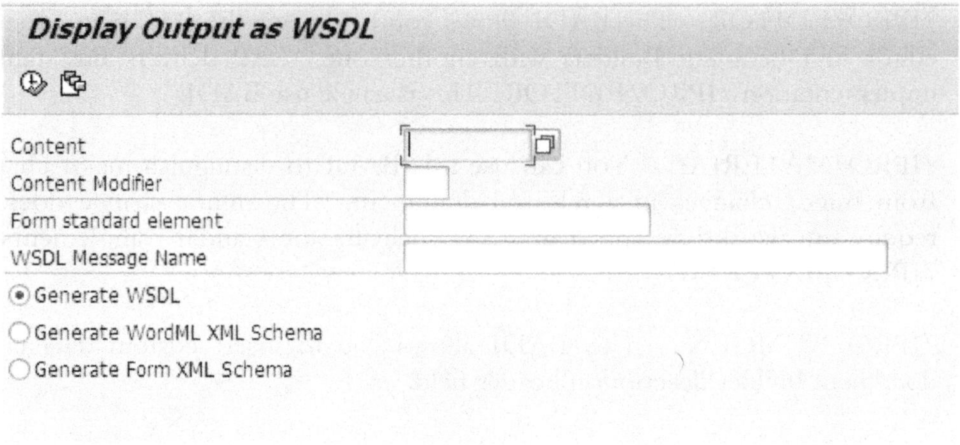

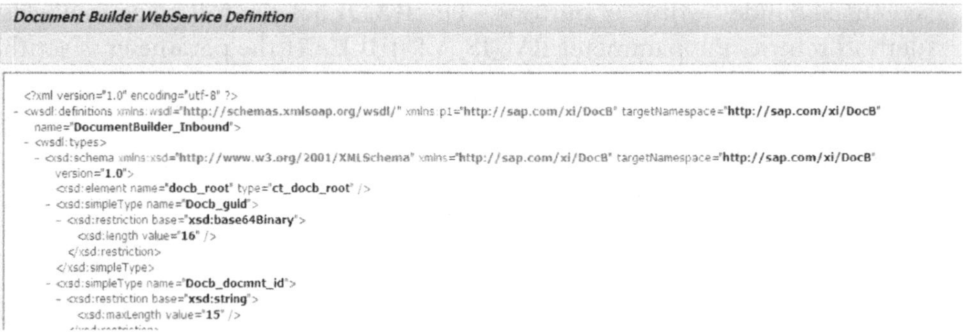

Download the field into your workstation.

- Build a new Adobe form interface using download file. The Adobe interface can be accessed by the transaction SFP.
  Create an adobe form interface.

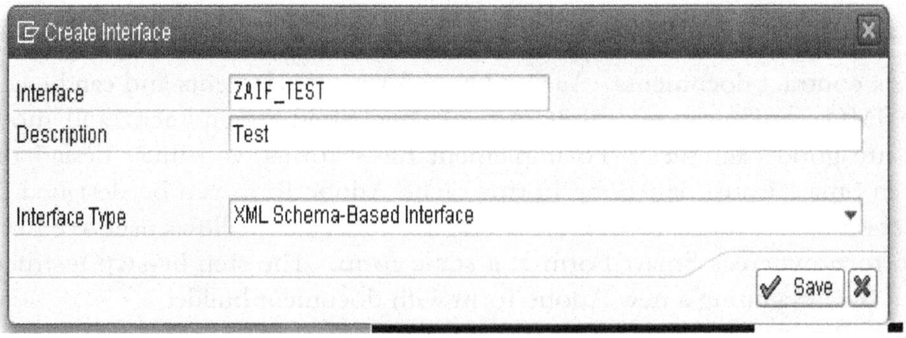

Load the downloaded file into the interface and activate.

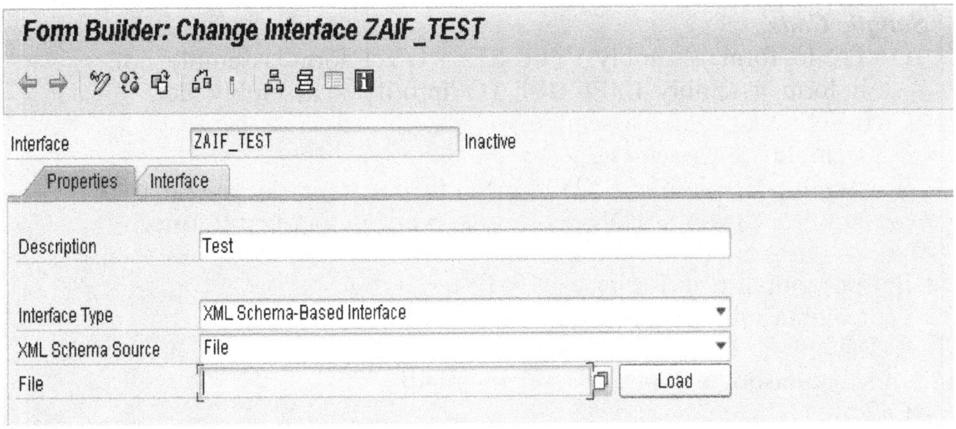

Design a new form with your form using a new interface. All variables are available in the XML interface and you can assign corresponding XML contextual into your fields.

- Define form elements and define form name at Text level. For example, if you are creating form elements for SF33 then create an element ZEF_SF33 with regulation and related rule ID. Create Text with text type 1 and enter the new custom form you created.

- Create a new ABAP class object interfacing /IPRO/IF_EX_ASSEMBLY_DEF. You can use the OSS Note 80703 for basic implementation code for the assemble process. Form method will execute the Adobe Form using the function module FP_FUNCTION_MODULE_NAME for the Adobe form defined in ZEF_SF33 element. There are number of transformation objects with document builders. You can use these transformation in the assemble process code.

- Implement the BADI /IPRO/OUTPUT.

Name: /IPRO/OUTPUT		Multiple Use: No	Filter: Yes
Description: Mapping for Synchronous Document Builder Integration.			
Method: GENERATE ***Description***: Generate the report output. Parameters:			
Name	Type	Data Type	Description
FLT_VAL	Import	/IPRO/TOUTDEF	Output type Filter
PIR_DOCUMENT	Import	/IPRO/IF_DOCUMENT	DOCb Document interface
PIV_DOCUMENT_MODE	Import	/IPRO/DOCUMENT_MODE	Mode - Display or Change
PRS_OUTPUT	Return	/IPRO/S_OUTPUT	Report Output structure

Sample Code:
```
DATA: lo_form_assembly TYPE REF TO zcl_form_assemble_pdf,
      li_form_assembly TYPE REF TO /ipro/if_ex_assembly_def.
CREATE OBJECT lo_assemble.
li_assemble = lo_assemble.
li_assemble->assemble( EXPORTING iv_doc = pir_document
                       IMPORTING ev_format = prs_output-text_format
                                 ev_doc    = prs_output-data ).
IF ( prs_output-text_format = 'HTML' ).
  prs_output-mime_type  = 'text/html'.
ELSE.
  prs_output-mime_type  = 'application/pdf'.
ENDIF.
```

3.5 Application Log

The application log is one of common logging used by SAP applications. Application logging records the progress of the execution of an application so that you can refer it later if necessary. Application log has the following advantages:

- System-wide uniform event logging
- ALV display support
- Analysis of Log data

Transaction SLG1 allows you to analyze the application log. You can use the transaction SLG0 to define entries for your own applications in the application log. Using the transaction SLG2, you can delete the log. The application log uses several tables to store the log formation. There ae function modules to read the application log.

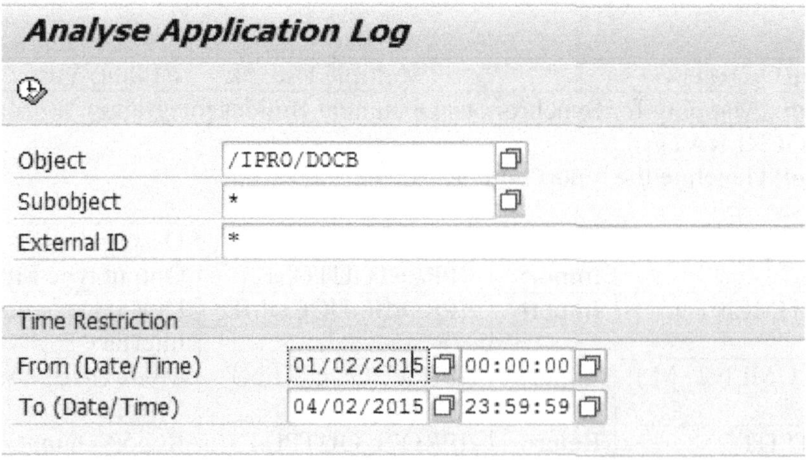

The Document Builder logs the application log under the object /IPRO/DOCB. Based on the application, the sub-object is used in the application log.

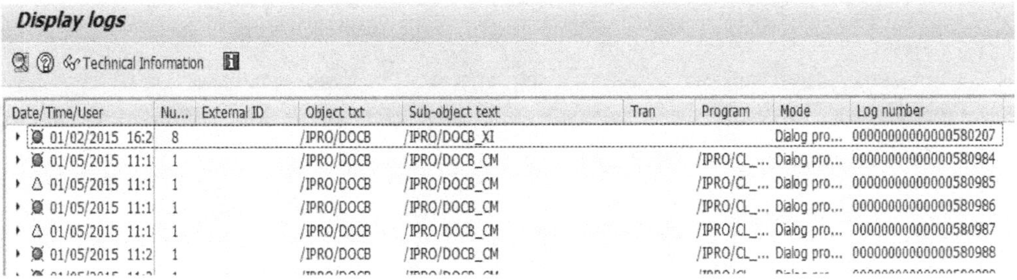
Display logs

Technical Information

Date/Time/User	Nu...	External ID	Object txt	Sub-object text	Tran	Program	Mode	Log number
01/02/2015 16:2	8		/IPRO/DOCB	/IPRO/DOCB_XI			Dialog pro...	00000000000000580207
01/05/2015 11:1	1		/IPRO/DOCB	/IPRO/DOCB_CM		/IPRO/CL_...	Dialog pro...	00000000000000580984
01/05/2015 11:1	1		/IPRO/DOCB	/IPRO/DOCB_CM		/IPRO/CL_...	Dialog pro...	00000000000000580985
01/05/2015 11:1	1		/IPRO/DOCB	/IPRO/DOCB_CM		/IPRO/CL_...	Dialog pro...	00000000000000580986
01/05/2015 11:1	1		/IPRO/DOCB	/IPRO/DOCB_CM		/IPRO/CL_...	Dialog pro...	00000000000000580987
01/05/2015 11:2	1		/IPRO/DOCB	/IPRO/DOCB_CM		/IPRO/CL_...	Dialog pro...	00000000000000580988

Make sure that implement the application log in your customer code. Use the application log /IPRO/DOCB and appropriate sub-object.

3.6 Reports

The document builder delivers a number of reports and few are briefly explained in the following.

- /IPRO/CLAUSE_COUNT_LIST – The report allows you to list out all active elements in ALV list.

- /IPRO/ELMNT_VAR – You can use this report to display all assigned variables to an element, content and regulation set.

- /IPRO/READ_SRM_VARIABLES – This report enables you to create simple variables in document builder. The report will call a web service in SRM system and receive the pairs of the variable name and data type. You can get the SRM system destination in the table /IPRO/TCONFIG with config name as 'LOGSYS_SRM'.

- /IPRO/DOCB_WRI - Create/Delete archived SAP document builder documents physically.

- /IPRO/DOC_EXPIRE – You can use this report to retrieve all documents that are due to expire and notify the responsible agent via e-mail. This report is associated with the workflow template document expiration WS40400011. You can use the report /IPRO/DOC_EXPIRE_PROCESS when the threshold value is set in the IMG configuration.

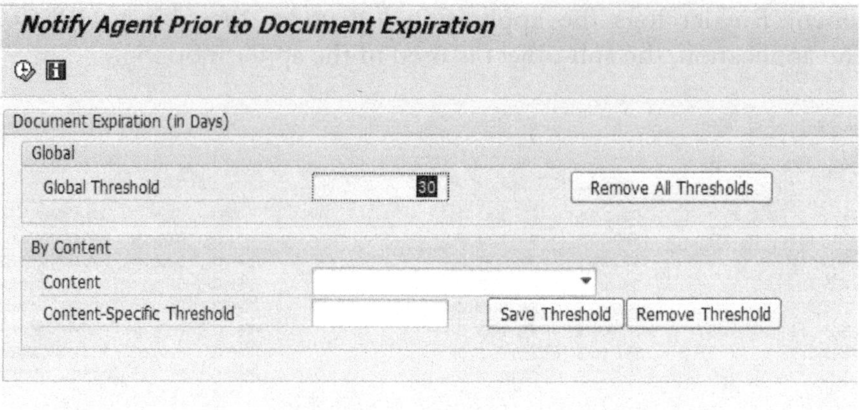

- /IPRO/CLASSIF_GENEATE – Generates characteristics and classes for the document. The application log are being created displaying messages. You can view the valid characteristics and classes in the transaction codes CT04 and CL02. The application log is under /IPRO/DOCB_CLASSIF of /IPRO/DOCB.

- /IPRO/OUTPUT_WSDL – You can generate the WSDL, WordML XML schema or Form XML Schema for given document content, modifier and element.

3.7 Authorization Object

The SAP authorization concept protects transactions, programs, and activities from unauthorized access. The SAP authorization concept is based on the basis of the authorization objects. Authorization object allows you to inspect your privileges for specific activities on the specific data object within a program.

The authorization object enables you complex checks of an authorization allow carrying out an action. An authorization object supports to group up to ten authorization fields that checked in an 'AND' relationship.

Function Module	Description
/IPRO/AUTHORIZATION_CHECK	Check DocB user authorization
/IPRO/AUTH_CHECK_DOC	Check DocB document authorization
/IPRO/AUTH_CHECK_USER	Check user authorization

Document builder provides the following authorization objects.

- /IPRO/DCSL – Authorization object used to allows user to execute specific parts of the document builder functionality. The defined fields are:
  - /IPRO/CTNT – Content Specifier

  - /IPRO/DCSL – Document Selection
  - /IPRO/COMP – Component of the document (Element, Template etc)
  - /IPRO/GRP – Group the component

- /IPRO/CONF - Authorization Object used to provide access to confidential document within document builder. The defined fields are:
  - /IPRO/CTNT – Content Specifier
  - /IPRO/DCSL – Document Selection
  - /IPRO/COMP – Component of the document (Element, Template etc)
  - /IPRO/GRP – Group the component

SAP provides authorization BADI /IPRO/GROUP_MANAGER to enhance the authorization validation. The BADI is additional authorization check only and it will not change from non-authorization to authorization. The BADI has only one method CHECK_AUTHORITY. The import parameters of the methods are Document content, Document selection, Component, Activity, Group and document. You can change the authorization flag PRV_SUBRC. If the value is not set then there is no authorization.

3.8 Search Help

Search help is a standard function and allows user to display the list of values (F4) for a screen field with the input help. In older times, it is called as Match code. The search help can be attached to a data element, check table, table field or screen field. SAP Document builder delivers a big set of search helps. The search help starts with /IPRO/H_.

3.9 Workflow

SAP Workflow is a workflow engine that enables the design and execution of business process within SAP application systems. You can use a workflow as a simple release or approval procedures or a complex business processes like Multi-Step Approval associated with multiple agents. The audit trail and history of system-based workflow helps the organization in a transparent manner.

The workflow is based on the business object repository types. The workflow can be triggered and terminated by the BOR object's events. A workflow must be defined before it can be executed. When you activate a workflow definition, you automatically generate a runtime version. When the workflow is started (manually or automatically), the relevant runtime version is used for the execution.

Document Builder provides you option to enable workflow based on the status of document. The possible statuses of the document are Saved, Changed, Deleted, Rejected, Approved and Expired. You can enable the workflow for these events.

All these events are part of /IPRO/CL_WF_DOCUMENT class object. The ABAP object has a number of methods include Set approved and Set Rejected. SAP provides option for Element User Status workflow. For this, SAP provides the /IPRO/CL_WF_ELEMENT object.

3.9.1 Workflow Templates

The following table provides the SAP delivered workflow templates for Document Builder.

Workflow	Description
WS40400006	One-Step Approval Workflow for Document
WS40400009	N-Step Approval Workflow for Element
WS40400011	Document Expiration
WS40400012	One-Step Approval Workflow for Template
WS40400019	0-Step Approval Workflow for Template
WS40400020	0-Step Approval Workflow for Document
WS40400021	Template Change Notification
WS40400023	0-Step Approval Workflow for Element
WS40400025	One-Step Approval Workflow for Custom Element
WS40400033	0-Step Approval Workflow for Custom Element
WS40400038	Workflow for Element User Status

3.9.2 Enhancements

SAP document builder workflow supports the following BADIs.

- /IPRO/WFL_APPROVAL – You can use this BADI to change workflow logic of the approval process. The BADI is 'Multiple Use' and SAP delivers the standard implementation /IPRO/WFL_APPROVAL. The BADI has the following methods:

  - CHANGE_DOC_APPROVER – Change approver for document or template
  - CHANGE_ELEMENT_APPROVER – Change approver for element
  - CHANGE_CUST_ELMT_APPR – Change approve for custom element
  - SEND_ELM_APPROVER_MAIL – Change and send e-mail to approvers.

- /IPRO/WFL_USRSTATUS – You can use this BADI to enhance the user status management.

- /IPRO/WF_ELEMENT_AGENTS – The BADI allows you to change element workflow agents.

Workflow Log – The runtime workflow consists of a sequence of work items which represents the individual steps. The work items are executed by the agent (dialog work item) or by the system (background work item). You can analyze the audit trail of the workflow execution using the work item log. You can access the workflow log using the transaction code SWI1.

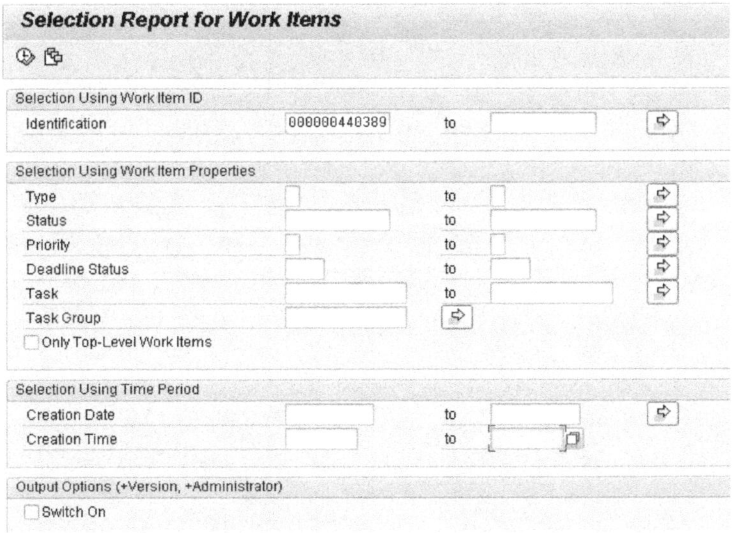

Event Trace – The workflow events are logged in the trace log irrespective of whether receiver called successfully. You can activate and deactivate event trace log using the transaction code SWELS. The event trace has triggering object type, triggering object, event id, triggering program and date. System logs the event only when event trace is activated. You can view the event trace using the transaction SWEL.

3.10 Troubleshooting

Timeout – Document Builder is time out when it assembles document. You can increase value of timeout in Internet Communication Manager (ICM) Settings. You can use the transaction RZ10 to setup ICM settings.

Variables – Make sure that simple variables are nested under a structured variable. When the simple variables are listed under the root, you cannot see variables in the XML schema.

Log-Off – When you close the document builder instead of Log-off, the document will be locked. You can clear the lock using the transaction SM12.

Made in the USA
Monee, IL
06 November 2026

67995733R00031